We the Kids

The Preamble to
the Constitution of the United States

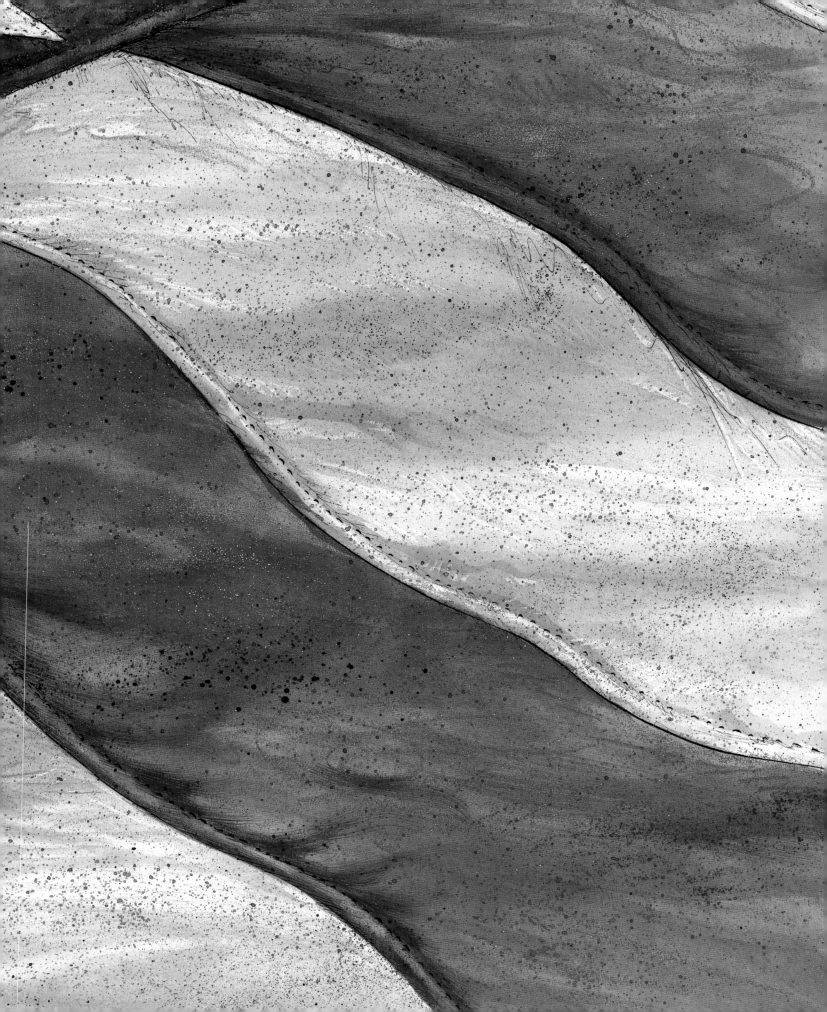

PUFFIN BOOKS

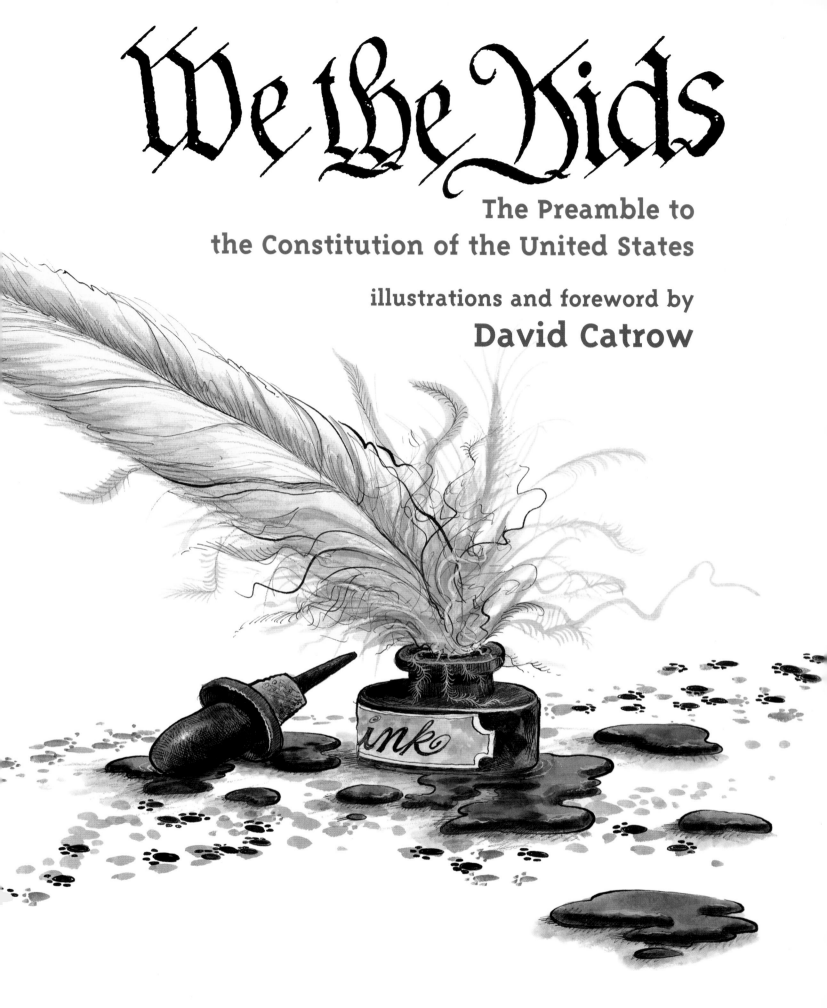

We the Kids

The Preamble to
the Constitution of the United States

illustrations and foreword by
David Catrow

For Deborah

PUFFIN BOOKS
Published by Penguin Group
Penguin Young Readers Group,
345 Hudson Street, New York, New York 10014, U.S.A.
Penguin Books Ltd, 80 Strand, London WC2R ORL, England
Penguin Books Australia Ltd, 250 Camberwell Road, Camberwell, Victoria 3124, Australia
Penguin Books Canada Ltd, 10 Alcorn Avenue, Toronto, Ontario, Canada M4V 3B2
Penguin Group (NZ), cnr Airborne and Rosedale Roads, Albany, Auckland 1310, New Zealand

First published by Dial Books for Young Readers, a division of Penguin Young Readers Group, 2002
Published by Puffin Books, a division of Penguin Young Readers Group, 2005
Designed by Lily Malcom
Text set in Triplex Serif Bold
Printed in China

40

Illustrations and foreword copyright © David Catrow, 2002

THE LIBRARY OF CONGRESS HAS CATALOGED THE DIAL EDITION AS FOLLOWS:
Catrow, David.
We the kids: the preamble to the Constitution of the United States / illustrations and foreword by David Catrow.
p.   cm.
Summary: A humorously illustrated preamble to the Constitution of the United States.
ISBN: 0-8037-2553-1 (hc)
1. Constitutional law—United States—Juvenile literature. [1. Constitutional law—United States.] I. Title.
KF4550.Z9 C38 2002
342.73'02—dc21
2001042350

Puffin Books ISBN 978-0-14-240276-4

The art was created using pencil and watercolor.

BIG WORDS, BIG IDEAS

The first time I was forced to think about the Constitution was in fifth grade. Presidents' Day was coming up and my teacher, Mrs. Baldwin, wanted to talk about BIG IDEAS!: stuff like FREEDOM, LIBERTY, FOUNDING FATHERS, PRESIDENTS. I sat doodling a picture of George Washington riding the red 27" Johnnie Ginger Mountain Ranger bike I hoped to get for my next birthday.

"WE THE PEOPLE OF THE UNITED STATES, IN ORDER TO FORM A MORE PERFECT UNION . . ." she recited, "SECURE THE BLESSINGS OF LIBERTY TO OURSELVES AND OUR POSTERITY . . ."

I remember thinking: MAN, why couldn't the guys who wrote this just use regular English?

"ESTABLISH JUSTICE, INSURE DOMESTIC TRANQUILITY . . ." But I guess that's just how everyone talked back in the olden times— like my grandfather, who always said things like "ripsnortin'," "hornswoggled," and "rooty-tooty."

I'm a much older guy now and I've figured out that our Constitution is simply a list of rules and promises written down by people just like you and me. Some were tall, some were short, some were thin, fat, or hairy, and all of them used to be kids. So you definitely don't have to be a grown-up to understand what they wrote.

For me, the Constitution is a kind of how-to book, showing us ways to have happiness, safety, and comfort. Sounds like common sense, right? But a couple hundred years ago those things weren't common AT ALL. For instance, back then if you said or wrote something and the people in charge didn't like it, they could put you in jail or stick tar and feathers all over you (ouch!). Now, even though a lot has changed, if you listen, the rules in our Constitution still make good sense— and tar is used to make highways and feathers are strictly for the birds.

A few years ago I went and saw the real Constitution in Washington, D.C. It's an old, brown, crackly-looking thing with curly handwriting that's almost impossible to read. But when it was new, it gave us rights and privileges that nobody had ever had before. It let us decide for ourselves what kind of life we wanted to have. At certain times I wanted to be a garbage man, baseball player, brain surgeon, and airline pilot. Instead I became a dad, an artist, and a political cartoonist. When I paint my paintings or draw my cartoons, I can do them any way I want. Being able to do that makes me feel very happy and very free. And I think that's exactly what all those old guys with their big words and big ideas wanted—for themselves, for me, for other grown-ups, and, maybe especially, for kids.

Catrow

The Words in the Preamble and What They Mean . . .

PREAMBLE: The first part of something, an introduction.

WE THE PEOPLE OF THE UNITED STATES: All the people in our country, including kids.

IN ORDER TO FORM A MORE PERFECT UNION: To come together and make things better for everyone who lives in our country.

ESTABLISH JUSTICE: To make things fair and honest for everyone.

INSURE DOMESTIC TRANQUILITY: To make sure we can all have a nice life and get along with one another.

PROVIDE FOR THE COMMON DEFENSE: To protect us from other people or countries who might try to harm us, as in a war, and to help us if we have been harmed.

PROMOTE THE GENERAL WELFARE: To help make life good for everybody. Having enough to eat, a place to live, being safe, and having friends and fun times are some of the things that make our lives good.

AND SECURE THE BLESSINGS OF LIBERTY: To protect our rights and freedoms and not let anyone take them away. Being able to choose our religion, to say what we think, and to get together with friends, family, and other people are some of the freedoms we have.

TO OURSELVES AND OUR POSTERITY: For kids, parents, other grown-ups, and all the people born in our country after we are.

DO ORDAIN AND ESTABLISH THIS CONSTITUTION: To write down, and then to live by, a list of rules and promises for our government to keep and our people to obey.

FOR THE UNITED STATES OF AMERICA: Our country—where we live.

These big words expressed big ideas.
Check out what the dog is doing in this story.
He will also help you understand what they mean.

We the People
of the United States,

**in order to form
a more perfect Union,**

establish Justice,

insure domestic
Tranquility,

provide for the
common defense,

promote the
general Welfare,

and secure the
Blessings of Liberty

to ourselves
and our Posterity,

do ordain and establish
this Constitution

for the United States
of America.

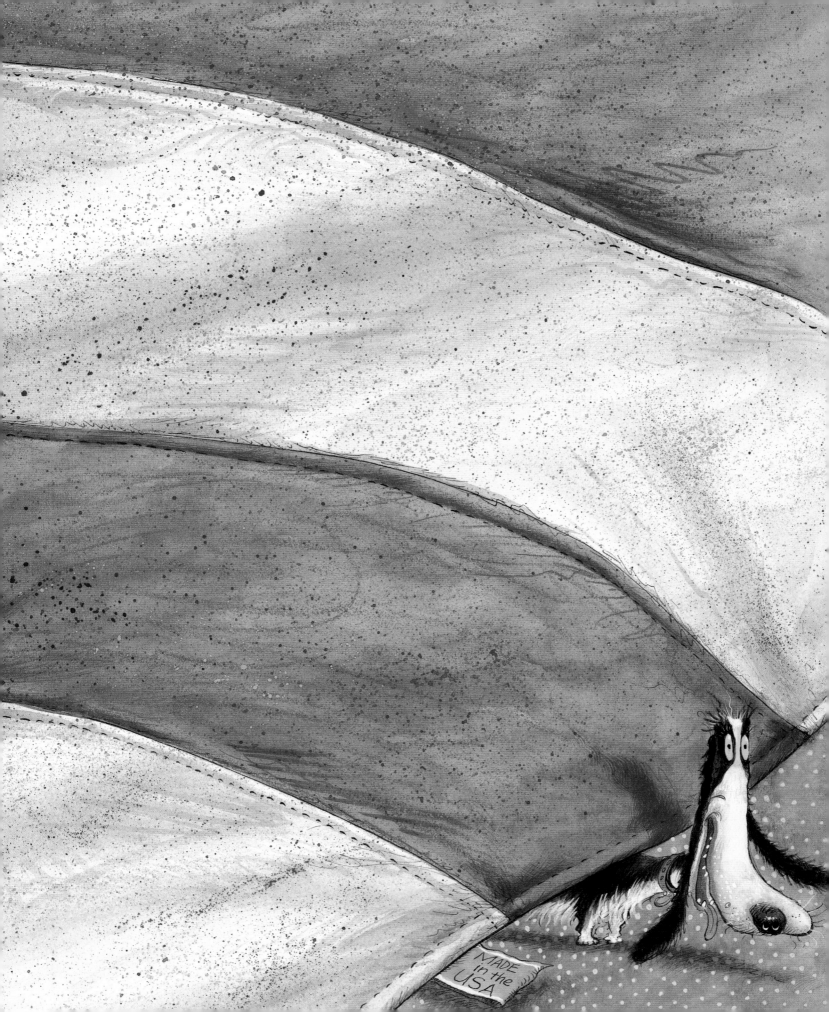